DATE DUE

MAR 1 2 1993		

SPACE SHUTTLE
CHALLENGER

Published by Abdo & Daughters, 6537 Cecilia Circle, Bloomington, Minnesota 55435

Library bound edition distributed by Rockbottom Books, Pentagon Tower, P.O. Box 36036, Minneapolis, Minnesota 55435

Library of Congress Number: 88-71720   ISBN: 0-939179-40-7

Cover Photo by: Bettmann Archive Inc.
Inside Photos by:
    Lief Ericksenn/Angle of Incidence: pg. 1, 30
    UPI Bettmann: pg. 5, 10, 12, 13, 18, 26

The Day of the Disaster

SPACE SHUTTLE
CHALLENGER

January 28, 1986

Written By: Sue L. Hamilton
Edited By: John C. Hamilton

NOTE: The following is a fictional account based on factual data.

SPACE SHUTTLE CHALLENGER

TUESDAY, JANUARY 28, 1986
11:37 a.m.

"T-minus ten, nine, eight, seven, six . . . we have main engine start . . ." The roar is deafening! Over a million pounds of thrust thunders through the vehicle. ". . . Four, three, two, one, and liftoff, liftoff of the 25th Space Shuttle mission, and it has cleared the tower."

It's beautiful, **Challenger's** engines blast forth giant white clouds of steam and smoke that quickly cover the launch pad. For a few moments, we lose sight of the craft, but then it appears — shooting skywards, heading for the stars. After all the delays, a perfect liftoff!

11:38 a.m.
Wait . . . something has happened. It looks like an explosion. It can't be. This can't happen. Are they coming back? A Return-to-Launch-Site Abort? Are the astronauts OK? *Are they alright?!*

This is the story of one reporter who followed ***Challenger's*** last flight from its hopeful beginning to its disastrous end.

FORWARD —
THE SPACE SHUTTLE'S BEGINNINGS

FEBRUARY 1967
The Presidential Science Advisory Committee suggests that research begin on a "reusable spacecraft."

MARCH 1970
Funding for the Space Shuttle vehicle program is approved. The Shuttle will act as a "space truck," carrying cargo (such as satellites) into space or returning with them back to Earth.

AUGUST 1972
Rockwell International is chosen to develop the Space Shuttle. It will cost an estimated $6.2 billion.

The Shuttle's design consists of three parts:

1. The Orbitting Vehicle, or "Orbiter."
    The Orbiter itself is the size of a small airliner. Measuring 122′ long with a wingspan of 78′, it weighs 150,000 pounds. Its huge 15′ x 60′ cargo bay can hold up to five satellites.

2. The Fuel Tank.
    Over 153′ long and 27′ around, this is simply a giant controlled "bomb" whose function is to lift the Shuttle into space. Fully loaded with liquid fuel, it weighs over 1½ million pounds. When the fuel is used up, the fuel tank drops off and breaks apart in Earth's atmosphere. It is the only part of the Shuttle that cannot be reused.

3. Solid Rocket Boosters.
    The two rocket boosters are 149′ long and 12′ around. Loaded with solid fuel, each weighs over one million pounds. At liftoff, they "boost" the Shuttle into the sky, giving it the extra power needed to reach orbit. Once fired, they cannot be stopped. After the fuel is used up, the rocket boosters break away from the Shuttle; parachutes open, and the boosters float back down to Earth, where they're picked up and prepared for use once again.

APRIL 12-14, 1981: MISSION STS-1 (Space Shuttle Transportation System-1)
Six years since the last American space flight, Orbiter **Columbia** goes up and returns. This is the beginning of nearly five years of successful Space Shuttle flights. Together, Orbiters **Columbia, Discovery, Atlantis, and Challenger** will fly 24 successful missions over a 57-month period. It almost seems routine.

REPORTER'S DIARY

FEBRUARY 1985
My job is to follow and write about the National Aeronautics and Space Administration's (NASA's) 25th Space Shuttle flight, Mission 51-L, which has come to be known as the Teacher-in-Space Mission. Scheduled for liftoff on December 23, 1985, one lucky teacher will be on board. 11,146 teachers have applied —NASA has a lot of homework to do to come up with one final winner.

JULY 19, 1985   THE WHITE HOUSE, WASHINGTON, D.C.

Vice-President George Bush has announced the winner: Sharon Christa McAuliffe. She's a 37-year-old high school social studies teacher from Concord, New Hampshire. I can just imagine her excitement. Now comes the work. She has five months to learn everything. It won't be easy, but it'll never be dull!

October 25, 1985

Mission 51-L's flight crew is now complete:

Commander	Francis "Dick" R. Scobee
Pilot	Michael J. Smith
Mission Specialist One	Ellison S. Onizuka
Mission Specialist Two	Judith A. Resnik
Mission Specialist Three	Ronald E. McNair
Payload Specialist One	Christa McAuliffe
Payload Specialist Two	Gregory B. Jarvis

Seven people make up the crew; the limit is eight. The commander, pilot, and mission specialists are all career astronauts with NASA.

Teacher in Space

Sharon Christa McAuliffe

The commander and pilot will handle flying the Shuttle. Commander Dick Scobee has already taken **Challenger** up in April, 1984. Pilot Mike Smith is a former Navy fighter pilot with many years of experience.

Mission specialists are in charge of the Shuttle's cargo. On this flight, Ellison Onizuka and Judy Resnik are placing two satellites in orbit: a NASA communication satellite and a Spartan-Halley satellite designed to observe Halley's Comet when it travels close to the sun.

For a regular person like Christa, the only way to get into space is to become a payload specialist. Her job will be to teach two lessons; one where she gives a tour of the shuttle, and another that covers the history and future of space flight. These lessons will be broadcast to millions of children across America.

Greg Jarvis, the other payload specialist, is on board to conduct experiments that will help his company in their work on satellite redesign.

Space Shuttle Challenger's

Back Row: L to R: Ellison S. Onizuka, Christa McAuliffe, Greg Jarvis, Judy Resnik.
Front Row: L to R: Mike Smith, Dick Scobee, Ron McNair.

Mission 51-L's Flight Crew

I think if I ever got a chance to go up, all I'd want to do is stare out of the Shuttle windows — look at Earth from way up there. Take pictures. Of course, being weightless would be fun, too!

Somehow, the excitement and adventure really outweigh the risks. Plus, NASA is so careful. There hasn't been an astronaut killed on a mission since Apollo 1 back on January 27, 1967.

DECEMBER 18, 1985
Mission 61-C, the 24th Shuttle flight, has been delayed, which means *Challenger's* liftoff will also be pushed back. They've rescheduled it for January 23, 1986. It'll give more time for training, but who wants to wait!

DECEMBER 31, 1985
Nine space flights have taken place in 1985. The Shuttle has carried more Americans into space than the entire Apollo program from 1968 through 1975! It's been a good year for NASA — 1986 should be even better.

JANUARY 12, 1986

After *six* delays, **Columbia** has finally launched. I don't know how this will affect 51-L's liftoff date, but it's sure to. Still, they'll have to get **Challenger** up quickly, otherwise they'll miss the best lighting conditions for viewing Halley's Comet with the Spartan-Halley satellite.

JANUARY 15, 1986

Senior NASA officials met today to discuss **Challenger's** flight readiness. There are a few "open" problems yet to be solved, but everyone is sure that it's a "go" for **Challenger's** flight.

JANUARY 18, 1986

Columbia has finally put down at Edwards Air Force Base, after bad weather twice prevented them from landing. This mission was jinxed — they couldn't take off and then couldn't land! Well, at least now NASA can get on with launching **Challenger**, although **Columbia's** late landing means another delay: January 26, 1986.

JANUARY 19, 1986

Several parts from the Orbiter *Columbia* are needed aboard *Challenger*. I never knew that NASA had only enough parts for flying one Shuttle. The parts arrived today, and immediately the technicians began installing them, *seven* days before *Challenger* is due for liftoff! How can they get everything done? And being so rushed, how can they be sure everything is OK? Still, they're the experts . . .

THURSDAY, JANUARY 23, 1986

It's a beautiful day here at the Cape — perfect for today's "Astronaut Arrival," when the Shuttle crew arrives at the launch site. Of course, this gives us reporters our chance to interview them. They're ready to fly. I hope the Shuttle is.

SATURDAY, JANUARY 25, 1986
11:00 a.m.

Launch-Minus One Day Review. All issues left "open" at the Flight Readiness Review ten days ago have been officially "closed." Looks like nothing will affect the scheduled launch.

2:00 p.m.

The crew has had their final preflight physicals and now they're in quaratine, unable to see anyone. No more interviews. I guess I can understand how they wouldn't want to catch someone's cold or flu right before they go into space.

9:00 p.m.

Bad weather is headed this way. This could be a big problem. The Shuttle can't fly in the rain, since at speeds of over 300 knots, raindrops hit the ship as though they're made of steel. In seconds, they can shred the 30,000 heat protection tiles that cover the Orbiter. It's hard to believe that these tiles, designed to withstand temperatures up to 2,750°, can't fly through the rain!

The Mission Management Team has a tough decision to make. If they go ahead with the launch tomorrow, Vice-President Bush will come to watch the liftoff. But if the bad weather comes in, they'll have to cancel the launch and his visit.

Space Shuttle Challenger sits upon launch pad. The shuttle has been postponed due to bad weather.

18

11:00 p.m.
The mission is scrubbed until Monday morning.
I'm going to bed.

SUNDAY, JANUARY 26, 1986
7:00 a.m.
It's a beautiful day — perfect for a launch. Well,
NASA had to make a decision, and it can't be
changed now. Let's hope the weather holds until
tomorrow.

MONDAY, JANUARY 27, 1986
1:30 a.m.
I'm staying up all night to follow everything. Cold
weather has come in. Still, they're moving ahead
with the launch.

The launch pad is deserted. It's strange,
disquieting to see the Shuttle abandoned like this,
but fueling has begun. It'll take over three hours
to pump the 500,000+ gallons of fuel into the
external fuel tank. No one is allowed on the pad
during this highly dangerous operation.

4:20 a.m.
The Ice and Debris Inspection Team is making certain that the frost on **Challenger's** tank isn't so thick that chunks could fall off during liftoff and damage the Orbiter's tiles.

6:15 a.m.
The Shuttle crew is sitting down to the traditional launch-morning breakfast of steak and eggs — the last "normal" meal they'll have for six days.

7:15 a.m.
"Astronaut Walkout" — the astronauts leave the building and march single-file past TV cameras and photographers to the waiting Astrovan. No time for us reporters, though.

7:20 a.m.
The Astrovan takes the crew to the launch pad. From there, the astronauts will take the elevator to the "White Room," where they'll be helped into their harnesses and helmets. Then they'll crawl through the Shuttle's hatch and work their way over to their seats.

8:30 a.m.

There's a problem with the hatch locking into place. Countdown is held at T-minus 20 minutes. More waiting!

9:30 a.m.

They've decided to open and re-close the hatch-locking mechanism. Astronaut Ron McNair, who is seated beside the hatch, will watch the pins lock into place.

The crew has been on their backs, strapped onto the Orbiter's hard, narrow seats for two hours. They can't stay like this for much longer. If the wait continues, they can suffer cramps, which could make it difficult for them to move in case they had an emergency after liftoff. I'm getting pretty tired of this, too. I've been up for 24 hours . . . let's go!

12:30 a.m.

First, problems with the hatch, and now, gusting winds have created a safety problem. Should an emergency arise where *Challenger* would have to return here to Kennedy (a Return-to-Launch-Site-Abort, or RLSA), it would be impossible for them to do so.

12:36 a.m.
The flight is scrubbed until tomorrow.

TUESDAY, JANAURY 28, 1986
2:00 a.m.
I'm up, but the temperature isn't. NASA's freeze protection plan is to allow the emergency showers and fire hoses to "trickle" all night to prevent frozen pipes. However, it's actually below freezing here (something almost unheard of in Florida), and now there's a thick layer of ice covering the launch pad. If there was a fire or fuel leak, the crew would have to run across glare ice to escape. Even the handrails are coated with ice. This really presents a danger of ice breaking off and damaging the tiles. I bet they'll have to delay the flight *again!*

6:00 a.m.
No word on canceling the flight. The crew is having their second launch-day steak-and-eggs breakfast. Everything is moving forward as it did yesterday; let's hope today it's worth all the effort.

8:25 a.m.

The crew is taken to Pad 39B once more to board *Challenger*. Although it's cold, the sky is clear — no sign of rain. Still, even from the press area, I can see ice everywhere on the pad. How will they be able to launch?

9:00 a.m.

The hatch has been closed and sealed. Everyone and everything is in place. We're waiting for the "go."

11:00 a.m.

The countdown clock is at T-minus nine minutes and holding. As much ice as possible has been removed by the Ice Team. Now it's up to the Mission Management Team to decide if the rest of the ice is still a problem.

11:15 a.m.

Good news! NASA has decided to launch! I'm sure the crew is glad that their long wait in those hard seats is finally going to pay off. New liftoff time: 11:38 a.m.

11:30 a.m.

The astronauts' families are up on the roof of the Launch Control Center. Other "VIP's" (friends, relatives, etc.) are taking their places in the bleachers next to the press mound. Usually, the VIP's are in another area, but over here is the best view of Pad 39B. I think it's fun for both the press and the VIP's to be together. We've all waited a long time for this launch.

11:37 a.m.

'T-minus ten, nine, eight, seven, six . . . we have main engine start . . ." The roar is deafening! Over a million pounds of thrust thunders through the vehicle. ". . . Four, three, two, one, and liftoff, liftoff of the 25th Space Shuttle mission, and it has cleared the tower."

It's beautiful. ***Challenger's*** engines blast forth giant white clouds of steam and smoke that quickly cover the launch pad. For a few moments, we lose sight of the craft, but then it appears — shooting skywards, heading for the stars. After all the delays, a perfect liftoff!

11:38 a.m.
Wait . . . something has happened. It looks like an explosion. It can't be. This can't happen. Are they coming back? A Return-to-Launch-Site Abort? Are the astronauts OK? *Are they alright?!*

11:39 a.m.
The Range Safety Officer has just exploded the booster rockets before they could fly back and endanger the coast. Still waiting to find out what has happened to the flight crew . . .

11:45 a.m.   Here's the word from NASA: "Flight controllers here looking very carefully at the situation. Obviously a major malfunction. We have no downlink (communication with *Challenger*). We have a report from the Flight Dynamics Officer that the vehicle has exploded."

The Space Shuttle *Challenger's* tenth mission lasts a mere 73 seconds. In an instant, the hopes and dreams of millions die, as American's space program comes to a fiery halt.

Nine years and one day after the Apollo 1 fire, NASA's 56th manned space flight has ended in tragedy.

There is no hope for the seven members of the crew. They have been killed. What happened? How could this happen?

EPILOGUE —
THE HALT OF THE SPACE AGE

JANUARY 28, 1986
Evening

Navy ships have spent the day searching the ocean for parts of the Shuttle. They'll continue searching to collect as much of the wreckage as possible to figure out what went wrong. It still doesn't seem real to me.

President Reagan delivered a tribute to the *Challenger* astronauts tonight. From his speech:
"I know it's hard to understand that sometimes painful things like this happen. It's all part of the process of exploration and discovery, it's all part of taking a chance and expanding man's horizons. The future doesn't belong to the fainthearted. It belongs to the brave. The *Challenger* crew was pulling us into the future and we'll continue to follow them."

FEBRUARY 1986

What happened? Here's NASA's explanation: there was a leak in the righthand Solid Rocket Booster field joint. If you look at pictures of the **Challenger** before it took off, you can see the smoke coming out. There were no warning signals; nothing to indicate that anything was going wrong. Fire erupted and burned through the External Tank. Fuel spilled out and ignited. Seconds after the tank had ignited, the Orbiter was ripped apart.

When the Solid Rocket Boosters are thrusting, there are no abort options. Neither the crew or the ground controllers could have done anything to prevent the disaster.

So, now we know what has happened. Somehow it doesn't make things any easier.

MARCH 1986

NASA divers have located the smashed crew compartment. The astronauts' bodies are still inside, strapped in their seats. Strangely enough, the forces that caused the Shuttle to break apart were not enough to cause death. Three "used" air packs have been found, proving that at least three crew members were breathing during the two minutes and 45 seconds the crew compartment fell toward the sea. However, the crew compartment hit the water with such force that no one could have survived the impact.

APRIL 29, 1986

The bodies of **Challenger's** crew are being flown out of Kennedy Space Center. They are going home.

All of the 14 missions scheduled after 51-L have been put on hold. A lot of work will have to be done before another Shuttle will fly. My story is finished. I hope the space program is not.

POSTSCRIPT

1988

Parts of the Space Shuttle are being redesigned. Plans are being made so that an accident such as **Challenger** experienced will never happened again. Seven lives were lost, but they have brought about changes that we hope will mean the saving of lives in future space flights.

If everything goes right, the Shuttle will go into space late in 1988 — almost three years since "the accident." Space exploration is dangerous. The unknown *is* dangerous — that won't change, but we can't stop exploring. It takes courage and determination to keep going. We'll remember Janaury 28, 1986 as a day of disaster that took seven brave lives. Yet, if their deaths are to mean anything, *we must* keep "reaching for the stars."

SOURCES CONSULTED

Billings, Charlene W. **Christa McAuliffe: Pioneer Space Teacher.** New Jersey: Enslow Publishers, Inc., 1986.

Joels, Kerry Mark, and Kennedy, Gregory P. **The Space Shuttle Operator's Manual.** New York: Ballatine Books, 1982.

McConnell, Malcolm. *Challenger:* **A Major Malfunction.** New York: Doubleday & Company, Inc., 1987.

NASA Public Information Office, Washington, D.C.

Report of the Presidential Commission on the Space Shuttle *Challenger* Accident, by William P. Rogers, Chairman. Washington, D.C.: Government Printing Office, 1986.

Waldrop M. Mitchell. "Research Council Critiques NASA's Booster Redesign." **Science,** July 10, 1987, p. 122.

Yenne, Bill. **The Astronauts.** New York: Exeter Books, 1986.